The
Life
We
Lead

Angel Anthony Cordero

MILTON & HUGO L.L.C.
4407 Park Ave., Suite 5
Union City, NJ 07087, USA

Website: *www. miltonandhugo.com*
Hotline: *1- 888-778-0033*
Email: *info@miltonandhugo.com*

Ordering Information:
Quantity sales. Special discounts are granted to corporations, associations, and other organizations. For more information on these discounts, please reach out to the publisher using the contact information provided above.

Library of Congress Control Number: 2024909670
ISBN-13:   979-8-89285-052-0   [Paperback Edition]
                979-8-89285-131-2   [Hardback Edition]
                979-8-89285-051-3   [Digital Edition]

Rev. date: 04/18/2024

"To my family, friends, mentors, and everyone else along the way: this is for you"

"Promise yourself to live a beautiful life"

Contents

Preface

This work is a compilation of over three years of experiences, memories, and lessons delivered through the wonderful medium of poetry. It covers a wide range of themes from love, life problems, motivation, society, religion, what it is like to be an author, and many more. I strongly believe that within these pages there exists a poem for everybody and anybody. I welcome readers from all walks of life to come and experience this wonderful journey of ours called life. I welcome everybody to come along and experience *The Life We Lead.*

THE TEN ORIGINALS

Time Lost & Memories That Haunt

It had been so long, yet it still felt all too familiar.

Fooling myself into not admitting the feelings I felt.

Oh! The time lost & memories that haunt!

That night her dress was the color of scarlet, but her words were silver.

The silver in those words cut my heart and made my soul melt.

Oh! The time lost & memories that haunt!

Yes, the night had started as she came with another.

They were not yet lovers, but more than friends and I a footnote with a painful, sad end.

Oh! The time lost & memories that haunt!

Yet as time passed a lingering thought did hover.

Could I change this story from long ago and make it have a different end?

Oh! The time lost & memories that haunt!

As the night progressed, I found my eyes wandering between her hair's curls and that bright ruby dress.

In my mind my thoughts ran wild and untamed.

Oh! The time lost & memories that haunt!

I sat across from her silent and reserved then she asked, "Do you want to dance?", I gave a shy yes.

In that moment my heart burned with passion and love.

Oh! The time lost & memories that haunt!

When we finished that dance, we both walked calmly back to sit where we had been before.

In fact, the rest of that night went too fast.
Oh! The time lost & memories that haunt!
I said goodbye to her that night with my heart feeling dreadfully sore.
I knew I had just lived a memory that would stay forever in the past.
Oh! The time lost & memories that haunt!
In the end, we both left in the same way we had come:
To different places, with different people, and different friends.
Oh! The time lost & memories that haunt!
Whether the story changes I care not, for it's all the same.
To be lovers or friends we still could have only one shared remembrance in the end.
Oh! The time lost & memories that haunt!

Confessions

So simple, yet different in a way too.
I see her and my heart jumps.
With each moment, I don't know what I should do.
This question my mind it stumps.
To confess would mean to expose myself to harm.
Not doing so pains my heart.
Rejection had never phased me until now.
Now I dread it with my soul.
"We are good friends and I think that's sufficient,"
My mind says to my wild heart.
My heart quips back as if to convince my mind,
"I want something that's more."
"I will pursue her even if she is blind."
My mind then quips back its own retort,
"Foolish heart, look now you're sore."
This argument goes on between heart and mind.
No rest as they pull and tug.
The fight is because my mind hears her words.
My heart knows what it has seen.
My mind listens to her soft words and deep thoughts.
My heart views her pull away.
All my senses tug at each other.
The truth is that I'm afraid.
This fear has caused my feelings to be covered.
With this my thoughts I had slain.
Loving is no fool's errand, even in pain.
I will love her more each day.
I could go on forever living this way.

Even then she will not stay.
She is the wind that can be calm or reckless.
She is not someone to keep.
She'll stay in my heart, but forever be away.
I can't confess my love for her is too deep.
Rejection I could not stand.
Wearing my heart on my sleeve bears a price steep.
I pay it each night I sleep.
Many have lived it prior.
Right now, I live as a hopeless young lover.
I hope for a fantasy.
Yet, I guess that at one time everyone does.
I hope for what cannot be.
I live in nostalgia of what never was,
Dreaming only to not see. Not even not to see but realize,
The lack of love in her eyes.
I'll keep these confessions deep and close to me
Far, where she will never see.
I'll hide them deep within my heart and my mind.
Maybe I will remember them for all time.
In the end, no rejection.
In the end, I will still feel lesser a pain.
I won't have to see her face.
I won't need to deal with her pain or mine:
Only my pain and that is fine.
If I never cause her any pain, I've won.

I kept her safe in my mind.
She can be happy somewhere else with someone.
In time I know she will find
Someone far better than I could be.
That day will come and I'll see:
I'll see her happy and grin far and wide.
My life done and then resigned.

Lighting and Storm Break (My Lost Self)

Should I return now? Maybe not.
Too electric, too forceful.
I move without a single thought.
This has caused me to rise and fall,
To rise and fall hard.
Life dealt me this deck.
I'm neither poet nor bard;
My life is a wreck.
I come without warning or time.
I pierce the clouds apart.
I'm the worst part of nature's rhyme.
No one considers me as art.
Lightning is my name.
I hold no great fame.

Silence

They know not the price of my silence.
To deny, disbelieve, and reject what I hold dear,
Fools, they wonder why my anger overtakes my fear.
They're blind, foolish, and tragically dense;
They lost me and my protection ever since.
They should be quivering for now their time has come near.
I'm back from the shadows; once again, I am here.
If nothing else, I'll keep my endurance.
They asked to be quiet, reject penance.
Now their lives are in my hand, they will cry every tear.
I hope they remember who backs me for He is here.
Call it freedom; call it a second chance.
Call this your warning, my warm and sad embrace.
If you still doubt me please run away I beg you, dear.
I will win this battle it won't matter if you're here.
Once I am done, I will leave here no trace.
Because once I am done only ashes have place.
Please leave now: my warnings are true, just believe me, dear.
This side of me I've hidden will cause you dark fear.
Staying here will cost you a heavy price;
Destruction is the cost for my true silence.
The full force of my backing turned against you all here.
I intend to leave after killing what you hold dear.
When I am done you will just know the pain of your sad
existence.

Your Blue Skies

Sorry I couldn't be there when you needed me.
If only they could have seen the me that you saw.
You took me for who I was and judged not my flaws.
We were only friends.
The blue skies above painted a story for you and me.
A story far different from the one that you saw;
In fact, our two stories had no common at all.
So much has changed from this place I must surely flee.
It hurts me to go, but I will stay in awe;
Of this blue sky that we looked upon and simply saw.
I'll look at it to remember you and maybe,
You'll look at it and remember me and my old flaws.
The sky will change so much between when we meet again;
It will ebb and flow and run and change like the blue Seine.
The story you saw had me staying here with you:
The story I saw running, as I now must do.
I'm so sorry that I must leave you now in this way.
Can't you see I would cause more pain if I stay?
Please look at that blue sky; remember me not with hate.
Because I'll look at it hoping to see you a different day.
I'm so sorry to not be there when you needed me.
I needed to go; I had a whole world to see.
If you still look up at that sky, know I do too.
I do it hoping that somewhere I will see you.
If it's nothing more than empty hope in my heart,
I'll still look up because as you said, "Cordero, the sky's a work
of art."

Finished

I find myself more melancholic than usual today.
Still batting, oh, for the millennium, just in a more painful way.
My mouth fully betrays me with the words that I say.
My mind has concluded to give up and go way.
My heart knows what it's about to go through: it's felt this before.
It knows that we've lost, and I'll be sore.
This story does not end with a bright sunny shore;
It ends with a sad man looking up at the sky evermore.
He looks at it as his thoughts fade to black.
This cruel world never cut him any slack.
He knows nothing but being stabbed in the back.
How many times this has happened he has lost track.
I lost count of how many friends I've lost.
Were my victories worth the cost?
I burned too many bridges I should have crossed.
Any chances I had—in the river they were tossed.
Now I sit here in the cold January air
Asking myself, "Why did I have to care?"
I rue the day when into her eyes I did stare.
It would have been better if I had never been there.
It would have prevented me the pain that I feel now,
Prevented me from asking myself "How?"
I know that she'll never love me now.
Still, I'll leave this scene of my life with a bow.
Not a bow that says "goodbye" or "the end."
No, it will be a bow saying "I'll see you again one day in another place, my friend.
I'll stay there with you on that day till Heaven for me does send.
My final gift to you will be my time, the only thing I'll have left to lend."

Contradictions

In flame, in fumes, in passion, in hate.
With cold, with ice, with ignorance, with pain.
In the dark, in the rain, in emptiness, in vain.
With light, with sunshine, with fullness, with gain.
In joy, in laughter, in smiling, in comedy.
With sadness, with crying, with frowning, with sorrow.
In forgetting, in regretting, in leaving, in going.
With remembrance, with nostalgia, with steadfastness, with
anchoring.
In rising, in winning, in succeeding, in celebrating.
With falls, with loss, with failure, with anguish.
In company, in gathering, in groups, in flocks.
With yourself, with solace, with one, with none.
In denial, in withholding, in hiding, in quiet.
With acceptance, with revealing, with openness, with noise.
In a mask, in a void, in nothing, in space.
With a bare face, with a completeness, with everything, with
reality.
In attack, in violence, in death, in breaking.
With retreating, with peace, with life, with rebuilding,
My mind runs all these options before each decision.
Yet many times it all runs opposite to its vision.
The contradictions of a mind that's been troubled,
A heart that's been buried under rubble.
These contradictions are the mask hiding the real me.
It hurts to say, but the real me gets stabbed every time I let
some see.

A Few Lines for a Friend

Your eyes tell better stories than any author:
The laugh whose song is sweeter than could write any composer.
A voice so powerful I can hear it in writing.
You feign and doubt when I say you're not annoying.
How you struggle to believe you're not a bother.
The truth is that you're like the sun.
You bring warmth and light wherever you go.
I honestly say that you're like the ocean,
The ocean of soft waves and soothing symphony.
I see you as a forest full of trees;
The trees are your friendship and a shelter to me.
You touch my heart as the wind touches my skin,
The wind that returns me to the present so I can feel alive.
I'm glad that you saw through my mask.
I'm happy that I can answer most of the questions you ask.
I do not hide myself when talking to you;
I know by now it's a foolish thing to do.
Hopefully one day you'll believe when I say you're not a bother.
And if you are a bother I rather be bothered by no other.
Know that as much as you see me, I see you.
I see the smiles you hold back.
I hear the words you don't say.
I know the doubt you carry.
The truth is we both have bones we bury:
Our buried pasts we choose to share now and then.
Yet through all this know, I will always love you, my friend.

Memories

We stared at the sky and the future before us.
We cared not of pain or sorrow.
The sun smiled at us as we thought past tomorrow.
We only hoped to borrow some of the life within the sky,
In this sky where a blistering sun over the trees had risen;
In a forest of the quilted and covered.
Here that blistering sun no one bothered.
The smiling, blistering sun too weak against the trees.
Through the cracks in these trees we saw the blue sky.
Through the breeze and the chill your eyes were like a pill,
The drug both keeping me tethered and pulled away from reality,
A tether hold as strong as the trees.
I know not why you had this effect on me.
I knew not who you could cause me to be.
All I know now is the memory of that day,
Today as I sit in a full room with nothing to say.
Why could I never say goodbye?
Why did I have to lie?
I regret having left that place.
At least I didn't see your face.
Your words as I left reflected too much pain.
Your words they flooded my brain.
Luckily, I do not remember your face that I did not turn back to
see as I left.
Luckily, I have forgotten your words.
Now all I remember is the sun, the sky, and the woods.

I Carry My Cross

Some days I remember myself in glimpses;
With those glimpses I almost remember my worth.
I remembered the frailty of it all.
Oh, how powerless am I time to stall.
The time passes and I'm pretty sure no one remembers me.
I could walk away, and no tears would be shed.
Forget me, this world is too dark and cold.
I am no longer young, no longer bold.
My will to fight has been drained by Father Time;
The talents given to me by Mother Nature are tired.
There's no one who I can tell my story:
It's better that way no true held glory.
I've been called arrogant, rude, abrasive, blind...
My mind is an enigmatic pattern that I hide.
They did not care when I showed them my heart.
I am a tired young man torn apart.
To those I've offended, I apologize, but I'm not sorry.
I felt love and sentiments, and I expressed what my soul knew as
true.
I may be tired, but I live as I please.
I cut the best flowers under the breeze.
My joy came in loving and hating and remembering and
forgetting.
There are no words I regret having said.
I look back on my life now with great joy.
I conquered life as a warrior from Troy.
Whether I was right or wrong, I'll let God judge.
Maybe I should have walked more and not cared as much.
At least I never lived in too much rush.
I carried my cross and now I will hush.

ABOUT ME
AND TO ME

The 1 & Only

He is the one who shakes the ground with his steps.
He steps upon treks new and all unknown.
The garments he wears tell nothing of him.
The him that everyone calls to carry.
It's always he who carries the weight of fate.
It's fate built into the palm of his hand.
One truth is that he cannot hold the weight,
One weight of all those who wait on him.
They hold out hoping he will be their pride.
They pride in all he has done so far.
Yet, he has always been so unsure,
Unsure of what the future can hold.
Why he is not sure he is not replaceable.
Why replaceable he cannot be, he is the 1 & only.

What a Wonderful Life

I sit on top of the mountain of my successes and victories.
The city which built and raised me below.
Silently the wind around me does blow;
It whispers a great many stories to me of good times that have passed:
These fantastic stories of simple love;
That love which flies freer than any dove.
Through all my trials God blessed me by making sure I have never been alone.
He gave me great friends around every turn,
Friends who saw my fire and helped it burn.
Now on this mountain I ask myself of any regrets I may have.
Well, I don't have any except for one:
I can't go back to relive what I've done.
Then again, I've never been the type to look back. I look forward.
I have a responsibility now.
My friends told me to keep winning then bow.
With the strength of God and in remembrance of them I'll keep going.
From the top of this mountain, I look down.
I struggle with the weight of this new crown.
Still I smile because I'm not alone; in fact, I may be home.
My new friends pushed me to be the best I can.
Empowered with hope I took my torch and ran.

A Mosaic of Hearts

Who am I? What is my purpose?
We tend to ask ourselves these lines.
Yet, it's hard to respond.
Well, here's how I'll answer:
I am a mosaic of hearts.
I serve to carry legacy.

The mosaic tiles left with me all my life
By friends through laughs, and enemies through some strife.
The tiles laid for the rest of time:
They're all a part of this heart of mine.
The pieces of their hearts that others gave me—
Well, now they are charged to me an eternity.

Since who I am is made of these hearts,
I am purposed to care for them.
Love given once.
A care unending.
They trusted me a piece of them.
Sadly, we found an end.

Even though we are strangers once again
I loved them as best as I knew how.
The time we shared I can't forget.
The tile of them forever is set.
I'll carry our moments all through life.
They'll comfort me when life is not fair.

So I'll carry all this love with me as I live.
I'll add a new tile for each new friend;
I know they will probably take a tile as well.
The tiles accepted, the ones given
Make a truly fascinating piece of complex art.
That art is a stunning mosaic of hearts.

3 Oceans, Infinite Adventures, 1 Me

Hello Pacific, they told me you never forget.
So as I swim in you I'll speak my life,
Keep these stories safe, so in time they'll be set.

Hello Atlantic, they told me you connect empires.
So, to you I'll charge those whom I love.
Keep them safe through life's fires.

Hello Mediterranean, you ocean of heroes.
In you I swam and pondered the future.
Keep still till I return to tell you of when I won and the cheers
rose.

Pacific, Atlantic, Mediterranean three oceans of different
characters.
To you three I charge the parts of my life mentioned above.
Parts of the endless adventures and parts of me that were
imparted from above.

A Letter That Won't Be Read

Hello there, younger me, my old good friend.
It's been a while. I thought we should chat.
Promise me you'll keep dreaming till the end.
Life has been best when we chose to do that.
The dreams you dream now, I accomplished them.
And yes, we did have help along the way.
Those that helped us were treated like gems.
Some came and went, but most were here to stay.
Promise me to not lose that bright smile.
And yes, sometimes we fell, but we got up.
Some things were hard, but they were worthwhile.
Just know goodness and mercy fill our cup.
So, even though you will never read this,
Young me, know that our life is filled with bliss.

How Did You Know?

Somehow you always knew
I knew what we would do.
So, you chased after those dreams,
Ah, chased them far and wide.
Yes, you ran us further than I imagined.
I ran us only to where you imagined.
Yes, but how did you know?
Somehow, I simply did.
I knew then as a kid
The future that I divined.
Dreams that they couldn't cap with a lid.
So, you lived our dreams, all of them, far and wide.
You charged full on ahead with God on your side.
Yes, but how did you know?
I guess it just happened,
Beliefs that were fashioned.
I was ready for the ride.
Dreams not left abandoned.
Somehow you fashioned and lived the life I dreamed.
Yes, I lived everything that dreamed and undreamed.
Yes, but how did you know?
I knew the same way as you now do.
Yes, but how?
Just keep living and you'll find out.

Year Gone By

What a great year.
Yes, I did quite a lot.
I lived without fear.
I loved and I fought.
Yes, this year taught me.
I remembered to dream.
Oh, the year taught me how to see.
I learned that things aren't always as they seem.
From one year to the next I grew.
It all went by so fast.
I saw a great many things, all of them new.
I loved this year that just went past.
What splendid times I had.
I lost some friends and made new ones as well.
In the end it was worth it, both good and bad.
I have new amazing stories to tell.
Goodbye, chapter eighteen.
Welcome, chapter nineteen.
And cheers to all the chapters whose stories remain to be seen.

Legacy

Let this my legacy be.
"He was a man who believed the world could be changed by just one life."
"He lived for the man who died and rose to set us free."

"He lived to serve and not be served."
"He dared to stand upon the word."
Let this my legacy be.
Let it be said that I avoided causing strife.
Let it be said that I loved.
"He lived for the man who died and rose to set us free."

"He invited those who others would cut down with a sword."
"He was faithful to Christ's Church, which is Christ's wife."
Let this my legacy be.

Let it be said that I learned.
Let it be said that I stood for only one accord.
"He lived for the man who died and rose to set us free."

I wish it to be said I served Him who gives life.
I wish it to be said I partook of grace given, but not deserved.
Let this my legacy be.
"He lived for the man who died and rose to set us free."

Passing the Torch

I'm used to being the go-to guy.
I'm used to everyone asking me why.
I know nothing else.
I know, however, that I must trust others now.
The torch must be passed.
Others now must carry the flame.
The weight was never meant to be mine alone.
It's time that I find another home.
Home for me is no longer here.
I won't disappear all at once, but simply fade.
My influence will become opaquer with time.
I'll head to wherever I now must be.
I see for once the flame burning bright without me.
The time has come for the next generation to rise.
I will pass this torch to you now.
With it I pass the weight of this charge:
Run far and run free!
Be truthful and honest and refrain from lies!
Care for others more than yourself!
Above all don't you ever quit—
Never, ever, say die!
Take this charge and care for it well while it endures.
The day will come when the moment to pass the torch will be yours.

Tell Me the Odds

Please, tell me it's impossible.
Go ahead, tell me I'll never do it.
Show me how stacked the odds are against me.
I beg you to show me everyone who's tried before and failed.
Please, tell me all the statistics you wish.
Go ahead, laugh at my dream.
By all means tell me that I can't win.
I beg you give me a reason to believe you might be right.
Do that and here's what I'll do:
I'll ignore you and press on.
Yes, I promise to wipe that smug grin from your face.
I'll do the very thing you said I never could.
Tell me the odds,
Tell them to me so I can show you why I'm that one in a million.
I'll be sure that when my work is done I'll have but four words
totaling ten letters to say to you.

The Artist

They were beautiful and kind.
Somehow, they always had the rhyme.
They were one of the few people to beat time.
From the moment they were born;
Until the moment they were gone,
They created feats of wonder that we all now look upon.

They created feats of wonder that we all now look upon.
They were beautiful and kind.
Until the moment they were gone.
Somehow, they always had the rhyme.
From the moment they were born,
They were one of the few people to beat time.

They were one of the few people to beat time.
They created feats of wonder that we all now look upon.
From the moment they were born,
They were beautiful and kind.
Somehow, they always had the rhyme.
Until the moment they were gone.

Until the moment they were gone.
They were one of the few people to beat time.
Somehow, they always had the rhyme.
They created feats of wonder that we all now look upon.
They were beautiful and kind.
From the moment they were born.

From the moment they were born,
Until the moment they were gone,
They were beautiful and kind.
They were one of the few people to beat time.
They created feats of wonder that we all now look upon.
Somehow, they always had the rhyme.

Somehow, they always had the rhyme.
From the moment they were born,
They created feats of wonder that we all now look upon.
Until the moment they were gone.
They were one of the few people to beat time.
They were beautiful and kind.
Yes, the artist and his legacy shall be kept in mind.

SPEAKING TO SOCIETY AND THOSE IN CHARGE

Flawed Values

We threw it all away.
Chasing material we stopped caring for souls.
We trashed what we should have saved.

There was a time we cared for our fellow men.
Yet, what did we do with that love and care?
We threw it all away.

Once we valued what money couldn't buy;
Now we value money and don't save our values.
We trashed what we should have saved.

There was a time when we hoped to make a better world.
Yet can you tell me what we did with that hope?
We threw it all away.

Once we saw people for their hearts, not their wallets.
Now we chase wallets and what they can buy instead of hearts.
We trashed what we should have saved.

The truth is all this buying and selling led to greed.
That greed was the seed for a tree that should have never been
sown.
We threw it all away.
We trashed what we should have saved.

The World Turned Upside Down

"See you in two weeks."
At the time, that's what we said.
Little did we know we might as well have said goodbye.
Goodbye to the world we knew;
Hello to what would become the new normal.
What happened is anyone's guess.
The interconnected world was forced to split.
All communication moved to a screen.
Faces were covered as emotions hovered.
Meetings we took for granted before were now a luxury.
There was far too much blame and not enough answers.
Experts were ignored by leaders.
Life as we knew it came to a halt.
The world turned upside down.
Life as we knew it came to a halt.
Experts were ignored by leaders.
There was far too much blame and not enough answers.
Meetings we took for granted before were now a luxury.
Faces were covered as emotions hovered.
All communication moved to a screen.
The interconnected world was forced to split.
What happened is anyone's guess.
Hello to what would become the new normal.
Goodbye to the world we knew.
Little did we know we might as well have said goodbye.
At the time that's what we said.
"See you in two weeks."

Where Have Our Leaders Gone?

Where are they?
Where are those who used to inspire?
Where are those who would march for change?
Where are they?
Where are those who fought for their beliefs?
Where are the ones who didn't turn back?
Where are they?
Maybe those who used to stand tall now hide.
Perhaps they got tired.
Most likely they quit.
Where have our leaders gone?
Most likely they quit.
Perhaps they got tired.
Maybe those who used to stand tall now hide.
The leaders vanished and Lord knows where.
They're gone now.
None are left.
Now we are left with cowards to lead.
They lead scared.
They lead poor.
Where are the leaders we admired.

How Many More

Have we really become this divided?
Is common sense really uncommon?
What happened to guaranteeing LIFE! LIBERTY! and THE PURSUIT
OF HAPPINESS!
Please tell me our leaders have not solicited themselves powerless
to stand against this!
Tell me, I implore you, that they have not become this cold!
When did saving life become so divisive?
When did acting on principle become so hard?
How does a party who claims to be for the little man let the little
man get shot?
How does the pro-life-pro-family party let lives and families
become severed.
Don't call for a gun ban while you stand behind them yourselves!
Don't say "Guns don't kill people, people kill people" if you don't
give the people help!
How many more times must we the people suffer for our leaders'
inaction?
How many more tragedies must we the people endure?
How many more times must we the people cry out, knowing no
change will come?
How many more times must we the people pay for what our
leaders in their cowardice and fear do wrong?
Washington was right in his warning of parties.
He knew we'd end up with our present.

He knew of our present in his past where he looked to the future all along.

He knew one day leaders would stop singing America's song.

How many times must you see us suffer before you act?

How many more times will you tell us to just be strong?

Please just tell us honestly if honesty is something you all still have.

How many more lives must be lost before you stop acting as merely republican or democrat?

How much more before you start acting as part of We the People?

Just tell us for once how many more.

We've grown tired of being shaken to our core.

The Words Behind Walls

We need to bring about change!
Yes, but how should we proceed?
How am I to know?
Well, your guess is as good as mine.
In that case, here's what I think we should do:
Let's keep saying that this time we'll finally act.
In fact, we'll even parade about a phantom plan.
Yes, they'll believe that this time will be different.
Then, just as soon as change seems inevitable,
Just when it all seems to finally go as it should,
Then we pull the plug.
We say there are more pressing issues.
We do nothing and keep our donors happy.
Even though the cycle is doomed to repeat, who cares?
When the inevitable happens, we'll just play the game again.
It's not that we don't see the tragedy;
It's that it's too uncomfortable to change it.
In order to change we would have to admit our wrongs.
Quite frankly we might have to work.
The control we hold could be erased.
It's easier to keep letting tragedies happen than that reality to
face.
Yes, you're right; I believe it's best if we lie.
Yes, change in exchange for power is not something I want to try.

A Disheartened Cry

Do you not see what is happening, or do you just not care?
You all have grown comfortable with your power.
Dishonesty such as yours is beyond compare.
Still, what do you care, sitting in your tower!
You all have grown comfortable with your power.
You forget it was we that chose you.
Still, what do you care, sitting in your tower!
Nonetheless, it's too late for us to start anew.
You forget it was we that chose you.
We're stuck with the poor leaders we've chosen.
Nonetheless, it's too late for us to start anew.
Sadly, our hands our tied and we're frozen.
We're stuck with the poor leaders we've chosen.
Dishonesty such as yours is beyond compare.
Sadly, our hands are tied and we're frozen.
Do you not see what is happening, or do you just not care?

The Table Forward

Some ask *why?* when they should ask *when?*
Others question when rather than how.
Many more ponder how over why.
Quite simply, many dreams are stifled due to this.
A great multitude of them quite simply die.
In a society so preoccupied with speed it's ironic.
The very thing heralded as a savior is now a downfall.
Rapidity has killed spontaneity.
It has tragically blurred the lines of truth.
Maybe then it is time to recognize
It is time to slow down and try to see eye to eye.
Maybe then the damage of asking so many wrong questions can be mended.
Perhaps some dreams can be revived.
Perchance spontaneity can return.
With luck the lines of truth could be clear once more.
So, hopefully, the question I end with now is right.
I pray the dream I propose won't be fickle.
When can we meet at the table to slow down and be honest with each other again to chase after all our dreams both vast and little?

THE LIFE WE LIVE

Overwhelmed

Some days living is bliss, others it's a chore.
This is the core truth we ignore.
It is not possible to be God.
He has the option to be everywhere at once.
Our mortal limitations cause us to choose.
Then how do we choose the limits of the time we use?
Do we choose our own deep passions?
Do we go where they ask for our time?
It's a paradox whose answer is never the same.
Seems life likes to play an unfair game.
We can't be at every good place.
Due to this we find ourselves wrecked, broken, hurt.
The choice is never an easy one to make.
Sometimes, the right choice causes us a smile to fake.
Still, we hold on to all hope.
Hope keeps us grounded, just like a ship is held to the shore by a rope.
We all know it's a good thing, maybe the only pure thing.
It's all we have; it's all we'll ever have to own.
Overwhelmed within our souls.
We're broken as life changes its tools.
In our brokenness we hope we make the right choice.
Overwhelmed, we listen to our violent inner voice.
We complete just another chore.
We choose because we cannot simply ignore that we have no control.
That overwhelming feeling of choice is reminding us all.

The Audacity to Dream

Are you audacious enough to dream?
Have you charged on when they told you it was impossible?
I dare you to be so bold.

You have all these plans, but no action.
You say, "If only," but don't believe you can.
Are you audacious enough to dream?
Take that "if only" and make it a reality.
Can you imagine the difference if you take action?
I dare you to be so bold.

Quit sitting there wondering.
Get up and start answering me.
Are you audacious enough to dream?

If the answer is yes, then charge on;
Charge toward all you've ever wanted.
I dare you to be so bold.

Besides, even in failure you do more than most.
You answer my question and hear my dare.
Are you audacious enough to dream?
I dare you to be so bold.

Let's Bring Cheers

Let the crazy dreamers dream wild dreams.
Let the poets write their poems.
Let painters paint again.
Let plays now be performed.
Let creation shine.
Let love invade.
Let it be.
Let go.
Let.
Let things be so you can see.
Let the crazy dreamers dream wild dreams.
Bring.
Bring them.
Bring them all.
Bring challenges.
Bring tribulations.
Bring on laughter as well.
Bring memories and bring laughs.
Bring the nights that will never end.
Bring the stories which become legends.
Bring on everything unexpected good, bad, and grand.
Cheers to the creators of legends.
Cheers to the mirrors they create.
Cheers to all the painters.
Cheers to all the poets.
Cheers to all the plays.
Cheers to the dreams.
Cheers to love.
Cheers life.
Cheers!

The Journey

What gets you out of bed?
What do you fight for till you're red?
About what do you dream?
Do you hold something in a high esteem?
If you know these questions, answers come along.
Come on this journey, though it may be long.
Should you come, I assure you your decision won't be wrong.
Your dedication will give you purpose.
It will help you break free from life's circus.
Then you shall always be at the surface.
Start your journey towards what you most want.
Once you start it, make sure to never quit.
Start your journey towards what you most want.
Then you shall always be at the surface.
It will help you break free from life's circus.
Your dedication will give you purpose.
Should you come, I assure you your decision won't be wrong.
Come on this journey though it may be long.
If you know these questions' answers, come along.
Do you hold something in a high esteem?
About what do you dream?
What do you fight for till you're red?
What gets you out of bed?

The Circle of Life's Language

If nothing else, learn this:
Learn the reason why anyone does anything.
It's simple and complex.
I'll even admit it sometimes doesn't make sense.
They'll give it all for love.
If nothing else, learn this simple lesson, my friend.
Learn this simple lesson if nothing else my friend.
They'll give it all for love.
I'll even admit it sometimes doesn't make sense.
It's simple and complex.
Learn the reason why anyone does anything.
If nothing else, learn this.
They'll give it all for love.
They'll drive themselves to ruin for love at all costs.
I've seen it many times.
More good people have been lost to love than to war.
Many more will be lost to love still.
Nonetheless, it's a good sacrifice that they make.
It's a good sacrifice that they make, nonetheless.
Many more will be lost to love still.
More good people have been lost to love than to war.
I've seen it many times.
They'll drive themselves to ruin for love at all costs.
They'll give it all for love.
Many more will be lost to love still.
Many more will fall into and out of love, yet.
They'll laugh and hurt more still.
Many more will fall into and out of love yet.
Please just learn this:
Love is bliss.

Unassured Assured Turnaround

The best is yet to come!
I assure you this is true.
For me and for you and for everyone anew.
The best days of our lives will soon be here.
So, when they arrive what will you do?
The best is yet to come!
I assure you it will be here soon.
Perchance today or tomorrow before the break of noon.
It is coming and that's all I know for sure.
I know this as sure as on a cloudy night I see the moon.
The best is yet to come!
I assure you that this I know.
Do not ask me exactly how I know, though.
Perchance it's just a feeling in my gut.
Nonetheless, I will follow where it leads me to go.
The best is yet to come!
I assure you, I'm sure of this fact.
It is not out of mere feeling that I act.
I'll chase this dream to the verge of madness.
I hope to reap from the faith I sow.
The best is yet to come!
The best days have not yet begun!

The Shadows in the Corner

They're not so scary once you step towards them.
In fact, they are reflective.
As you analyze them, you gain perspective.
Facing them provides new freedom to you.
Yet after you face them comes a mystery of which you are
detective.
They're not so scary once you step towards them.
The difficulty comes in taking that step.
Depending on the step, your throat tightens as if infected by
strep.
You'll be so careful not to make a mistake in the unknown.
Yet after you first move it becomes easy not to misstep.
They're not so scary once you step towards them.
In fact, you come to recognize they're powerless to hold you
down.
As you take them on, you find they're easy to drown.
Their weight was never anything more than an illusion.
Yet for some unknown reason, you gave them a crown.
They're not so scary once you step towards them,
The shadows in the corner that represent your fears.
If you'll be so bold as to try, you'll beat them and move on;
You'll see there's no need to live with the fears that cause your
tears.
They're not so scary once you step towards them.
No, they were never meant to be frightful at all.

Unnoticed Till It's Gone

The frailty of it will cut through a room.
It's easily broken, but washes over people like a monsoon.
There are those who beg for it.
There are those who run from it.
It's able to encompass a whole room.
Still, even the wind can kill it.
The birth of it always comes after the loudest moments.
The death of it almost always comes as a whisper.
In some moments it invokes peace.
In other moments it invokes anguish.
Some beg for it to be broken.
Some clamor for it to be instilled.
Oftentimes, it goes completely unnoticed.
Oftentimes, it will go on not existing for days.
Yes, it is unnoticed until it is gone.
Yes, the presence of silence is not felt till it has left.
Yet, in the moments it exists it holds a moment like nothing else.
It's silence that holds the moments where we reflect on ourselves.

Breathe, Just Breathe

I find myself in awe of the beauty of life.
Then I wonder how many times I've rushed by without
appreciating it.
The beauty of life is that it exists in a perfect tense.
Like its creator this beauty is, was, and will be.
The light which I take for granted,
The flowers I don't stop to smell,
The wind whose sound I ignore:
All of this beauty and so much more.
People tell me beauty fades, but I do not believe this to be true.
The beauty of life does not fade;
The beauty of life just transforms into something new.
In spite of me that light becomes the warmth on my face or the
kiss of the moon.
Those flowers I did not stop to smell become autumn's infinite
color-changing sea.
The wind I did not listen to becomes the vessel by which music
travels.
So, as I stop for a moment I come to see and believe.
I believe that life is eternally beautiful if only I take some time to
breathe, just breathe.

The Eternal Question

Who am I?
Three words asked eternally with no response.
Some say we are our own identity.
Others say we are who others claim us to be.
Then more say we are a mixture of these two views.
What if each of these thoughts is right, though?
To ourselves, we are the hero of the story we author.
To others we are who they need us to be for their story to progress.
In solitude to our subconscious, however, it becomes clear that our identity evolves and changes.
So here is what I answer to those three age-old words:
I am who I claim to be.
I am also who others see me to be.
I am neither a hero nor villain nor anything else forever.
The truth is I believe my identity has and will continue to evolve.
Yes, I don't believe identities were meant to be fixed.
Like life they were meant to evolve.
The beauty of being human is that our nature can change.
That's why those three words have no fixed answer.
I doubt they ever will.
So, while the debate may rage on for others seeking an answer,
I've decided to be part of it no more.
I've decided to live my life and just let my legacy and identity figure themselves out.
I've decided that answering those three words is something I no longer wish to worry about.

In Time

Live each moment in the way you desire.
Take each breath at the pace you set.
Don't fear stepping into the fire.
Regret is more powerful when it pertains to what was not.
Failure is a possibility, yes.
Success, however, is one as well.
It is true that the troubles of today will pass.
When they pass a new day has come and dawned.
A better reality is the one you wanted to live.
At least this reality is your own choice.
Yes, things may happen, and you will react;
Yes, the choice of your reaction may be frightening.
Yet is that not what life is?
For what would life be if you knew the destination of all your
turns?
So even if you're not entirely certain, I implore and charge you
this:
Step towards the fire and don't hold your breath.
Chase your heart at the pace you wish to set.
In time, all the apprehensions and worries fade.
In time, all you'll have left are the memories you made.

The Novel of Life

Each of us is a grand novel in the library of history.
Some of us are layered novels.
Others are blank and direct.
Some of our novels tell the story of our life alone.
Other tell not just our stories, but also of those who helped us write them.
The odd fact of these novels is that none of us truly dictate or write them.
The stories within them are written by those who come to know us.
For it is they who write wholeheartedly what they believe us to be.
So, it then is also true that not one of us has our full story in just one novel.
No, the library of history holds a novel distinct for anyone we've ever influenced, and the novel we write about ourselves.
In the end, all the library's novels are then bound together in one great book which is "The Novel of Life."

A MESSAGE FROM TIME

The Most Unremembered Time

You didn't recognize me then.
How could you, being so small?
I am time you know; immense and all.
I'm hard to recognize in that first stage of life.
Why, at the time you hadn't even witnessed the sun fall.
You didn't recognize me then.
I remember how sheltered you were.
I remember your peace I didn't want to stir.
Yet, regardless of my wishes, eventually I did stir your peace.
It was impossible for me from my path to deter.
You didn't recognize me then.
Yet, part of me had always known you.
Even then I knew what you would do.
Infantile as you were with so much potential,
Though you didn't know it, I knew the doors you would one day
walk through.
You didn't recognize me then.
I passed by you in a flash.
I was gone like a runner breaking in a dash.
Your infant age was gone when you came to know who I was.
That infant age of yours was blown in the wind like ash.
You didn't recognize me then.
Oh no, you didn't recognize your friend time then.

Folly of Youth

The Folly of Youth
Takes place in three stages.
The cycle has held up through the ages.
Yes, it's a cycle which has held for all of time.
So intrinsically wound is it to become their cages.
The Folly of Youth
As schoolboys and girls learn society's rules,
They're told smart people hold these rules like jewels.
And even though many rebel against the structure,
Most learn to make the rules their tools.
The Folly of Youth
It makes them think they're invincible.
They forget they're all too visible,
So, they charge carelessly with no regard.
They laugh at challenges no matter how formidable.
The Folly of Youth
They're still young, but now they've aged.
The setting for the rest of their life is staged.
All they've done from schoolboy to now flashes before their eyes.
They see time for how fast I am; now they've realized.
The Folly of Youth
Yes, that's The Folly of Youth.

The Cry of Middle Age

There's half gone and half left.
I've seen this age trashed and I've seen it bloom.
This is the first age they recognize fate's loom.
I've learned to both love and hate this age.
I love when they build life and hate their groom.
There's half gone and half left.
Some of them build wonderful lives at this stage.
Others act as if they're in a cage.
I have never really understood their choices.
All I know is seeing them waste this stage causes me rage.
There's half gone and half left.
They're not as nimble anymore, but they're still spry.
Thank goodness that they as an infant no longer cry.
I've seen them pass infancy and youth into this middle age.
This stage in years is long, but during it I will fly.
There's half gone and half left.
In the end, I'll tell the story of the middle.
Their friend time will answer that old riddle.
When this age is done, they'll be able to answer whether the glass
was half empty or half full.
At the close of this age, my existence with them will be brittle.
There's half gone and half left.
I hope they'll focus more on what's left.

Nearly a Full Story

I wish I lasted longer in this age.
Wisdom now fills their old bones.
Now I see them move like stones.
The years we shared lay heavy on their bodies.
Every time they move now, I hear groans.
I wish I lasted longer in this age.
As I passed, they became old.
Now they are no longer as bold.
Most days they just remember the past.
They remember the past and all the stories they told.
I wish I lasted longer in this age.
Now they just pass on what they've learned.
They give away what they've earned.
They try to lead others away from their mistakes.
I just stood by as those hands measuring me turned.
I wish I lasted longer in this age.
Together both them and I are running out.
The realization of this is a drink rather stout.
Neither they nor I can do anything about it.
The fact of that is rather sad, no doubt.
I wish I lasted longer in this age.
I'll miss them when the next one comes.

Time's Sign-off

Goodbye, my friends.
Ah, I flew by too fast.
Once, just once, couldn't I last?
I always believe this age comes too soon.
I watch another of you become the past.
Goodbye, my friends.
Congratulations on lives well spent.
I wish this age I would be able to prevent.
Unfortunately, that power is above me.
More of me to you cannot be lent.
Goodbye, my friends.
I wish you well as you move outside my grasp.
Though, onto you longer I tried to clasp,
I had no strength to hold you here.
I'll miss you as you leave with a final gasp.
Goodbye, my friends.
Your final age has more power than I.
History has proven this is no lie.
Though I wish it wasn't true;
Sooner or later, I run out and you die.
Goodbye, my friends.
You all moved through me and affected my sacred line in
the end.

THE TIMES

An Ode to the Past

Some say to forget you;
Others dictate to learn your lessons.
As for me, I choose both.
I'll forget the times you made me cry;
I'll remember where I cried and why.
It's best I forget loves gone wrong.
The song of what went wrong I'll always recall.
I'll recall the fall of the final note you wrote.
Oh, Past, I lied saying you didn't interest me.
I was simply too blind to see.
Without you, I wouldn't be who I am.
Memories of you help me make better decisions today.
You won't stay forgotten by me, but remembered.
I won't forget you through the hustle and bustle of life.
I'll keep the lessons you taught me sharp as a knife.
Nonetheless, I might forget people who were part of those
lessons.
We'll just have to see what happens when the future beckons.

An Elegy to the Present

It's funny how you were both alive and dying at the same time.
Controllable for a moment and then you were gone.
I wish our moment would have had longer to last.
Nonetheless, present you were a gift to me.
You were a gift once and once again will you be.
Present, oh, you who became the past:
Your time lasted a time far too short.
Yet maybe that's why you were a gift.
You were a gift because of your fleeting nature.
You were a gift not meant for later.
Maybe I should have treasured you more,
Because the moment you died was abhorrent.
I wish someone would have told me how much I would miss you.
I wish someone would have told me letting you fly by was a mistake.
Even if they had said so I would probably have passed over their words like leaves with a rake.
What made you a gift was that you passed so fast.
I only wish I would have loved you before you became the past.

A Call to the Future

You're the most elusive of my understanding of time.
The nature of you is very different from who I am.
Yet, somehow, I can affect you but never know how or why.
Future, you're always in motion;
But, for all your power, one bad choice of mine causes your erosion.
For your sake, I try to make the right choice.
Unfortunately, you have no voice to tell me what to choose.
I'll simply have to hope I choose right and wait to meet you.
Sadly, I won't meet you cause if I do you become the present.
Although meeting you before you became the present would be pleasant.
I know, nonetheless, that is not possible.
The fact I don't know you is what makes you, you.
You're the future because I can change you without knowing.
So even if we never meet,
I'll walk along to the beat.
I'll keep singing a song to you that I hope you'll call:
He was the one who always gave it his all.

MY FAMILY

Us

She, she guides us all.
Our home is in her image.
She is mom and wife.
He, he leads us forth.
He dictates how we all move.
Father and husband,
He, he makes us smile.
Youngest of us, full of life.
Brother and son,
He, he calculates,
Checks our decisions for us.
Big brother and son.
We are family.
Always have and we shall be,
For eternity.

The Hardest Worker I Know

Of course, you work.
The expanse of your triumphs dwarfs those who criticize you.
It's fools who think you don't work.

You raised a family into an empire.
Your critics saw their faux cities crumble.
Of course, you work.

You brought forth two purpose-filled kings.
Your critics raised knaves and cowards.
It's fools who think you don't work.

You are a rock firm and immovable.
Your critics can't even stand on their own.
Of course, you work.

You are strong as birch and gentle as rose.
Your critics are weak as sand and rough as gravel.
It's fools who think you don't work.

You are the best of us, and you always will be.
Your critics work only to fake being what you naturally are.
Of course, you work.
It's fools who think you don't work.

Me

I'm a singer who can act.
Maybe an actor who can dance.
Probably a dancer who can tickle the ivories.
Perhaps a pianist who can write.
Most likely a writer who can draw.
Finally, an artist who's made nothing of notice at all.

I'm a son who loves and is loved.
I'm a brother who makes time he doesn't have.
Maybe a friend to those who know me.
Most likely an enigma to those who don't.
Above all a person who cares too much in this careless world.

I'm a fighter who stopped fighting,
Maybe a lover who stopped loving,
Probably a warrior with no war left for him,
Perhaps an old soul placed out of time.
Most likely a dreamer who just can't realize his dreams just yet.
Finally, a young man who knows the future is not set.

I'm he who does what he feels.
I'm he who says what he means.
Maybe sometimes I tried to do too much.
Most likely I couldn't feel so I tried to touch.
Above all I did and still do what I feel is right.
I'm all the things here that I say I am.
I am now and hope to always be a creative, assertive, caring, loud,
outgoing, and honest man.

Millionaire Smile

One September Tuesday,
It was the month's last day,
An answer to a prayer arrived.
He brought a timeless smile to life.
It was the month's last day,
With it came an eternal memory.
He brought a timeless smile to life.
Truly, that smile was a gift from God,
With it came an eternal memory.
The smile that could light the darkest night,
Truly that smile was a gift from God.
It has served well through highs and lows.
The smile that could light the darkest night.
A smile to be carried among the stars.
It has served well through highs and lows.
The smile of the best brother I could ask for arrived.
A smile to be carried among the stars.
An answer to a prayer arrived.
A smile of the best brother I could ask for arrived
One September Tuesday.

The Words I Sometimes Fail to Say

You have led me well without fear.
Never once did you leave my side.
Through good and bad you were right here.
My needs have always been supplied.
You are both my rock and my spear.
Above all, you have been my guide.
Thank you for everything you've done.
I am honored to be your son.
Through all my days and existence,
You've been part of all I have won.
You always gave me assistance;
You went for me when from my purpose I would run.
I learned much from your persistence;
I will learn more with each new sun.
Thank you is not enough to say.
Still, it's the right word for today.
Thank you for all you have done.
I'm blessed to be your son.

Who I Can Only Hope to Be

First, a man who loves God above all.
A man who puts his family above himself.
All-encompassing a man who leads.
A man who never finds excuses.
A man who never shies from problems.
A man who is firm in his beliefs, but always willing to learn.
The simple principle of a man such as this.
Yes, here's my wish.
I wish that the man who has shown me the man I want to be gets many years so he can see.
Yes, I want him to see that whatever I accomplish is because of all that he has taught me.

PILLARS

Guide For When You're Down

Yearn for the best, for this is right.
Open your thoughts and mind and sight.
An unequivocal victory should be your goal.

So, what is it that you are waiting for?
Have you no faith, no hope in who you are?
Obtain all your dreams—I didn't think you were a quitter.
Ultimately, what or who can stop you?
Life is only one: what will you make yours?
Doubt and fear cast them out. You're not meant to carry them.

Believe in yourself, because if you don't no one else will.
Every day remember that favor and mercy are new upon you.

After everything remember to be humble and kind.
Never forget to smile and tell people you love them.

Onward and upward always be the head and not the tail,
Verily you are above and never beneath.
Every time you enter or leave you are blessed.
Righteous victory is guaranteed unto you.
Completely believe in the promise of who you are and never
doubt.
Overcome what troubles you and never quit.
Move-in the promise of who the Lord made you to be.
Every day sing His praises up high.
Reach for the stars and make sure to fly high.

1 Line Reminders

Hope: you must never let it go.
Every day remember His mercies are new.
His thoughts are higher than your thoughts.
Ahead of you is the future He ordained.
Speak life into every situation.
Add joy to every place you go.
Hope: you must never let it go.
"Overcomer," that is your title.
Promise yourself to always strive for better.
Eternally and perpetually fight for what is good.
Ahead of all else, dream big.
Never be so afraid to fail that you don't try.
Driven and purposeful is the way to live.
Add courage to your soul and mind.
Faith will guide you.
Unseen fantasies will become your legacy.
Teachable is the best way to be.
Ultimately, live within your purpose.
Reach for the stars even when they seem unreachable.
Every day is a day to become better, even if by 1%.
Fearless living is quaint yes, but also the best.
One step at a time is better than no progress at all.
Reaping and sowing, that law still stands.
You may go down, but you won't go out.
Only you can build your future, so build a good one.
Unique, holy, and righteous is how you should see yourself: God sees you as such.
You were made that way by the finished work of His son on the cross.

Prosperity

Laid in the grave He would not remain in.
In glorious fashion three days later, He would rise.
Fulfilled was The Passion of Christ.
Eternal life that day was bought with His blood.

Ah, but there's more than just life after death.
No, He is not a God of "just enough."
Delve into His word and see.

Love led Him to the cross.
It was love that raised Him from the dead.
Forever seated on the throne, our savior is He.
Even when we don't see it He is still working.

Made was the covenant in blood,
Ordained by the Father in Heaven above.
Righteous and redeemed we are now in His sight.
Endings for us are now new beginnings.

Abide in Him as He now abides in you.
Believe now that you can have an abundant life.
Until He returns you are charged with His word.
Never forget what He died to give you.
Death for Him was the sacrifice for your abundant life.
And when He rose, your life was secured here and in Heaven.
Never doubt the power of the blood.
Truthfully, I say to you;
Life was meant to be lived abundantly.
You now can go live in this truth.

In the Storm

Even when I've been down, I was never out.
Viciously I fought to rise again.
Every moment, I kept my eyes turned towards Heaven.
Never once did I consider quitting.

In the middle of the storm, I will praise You.
Not once has Your word returned void.

The best is yet to come.
Holy I hope to walk in Your sight.
Entirely, I place my faith and trust in You.

Storms may come, but You will calm them.
Triumphant for all time You stand.
Oh, even if I walk through hell I fear no evil, for You are with me.
Reaching out my hand, I'll walk in love as You commanded.
Mighty and strong above all are You, Lord God.
So, forever will I say worthy is The Lamb.

Of course, I will worship You only;
For You alone can save.

Life will have its troubles, but You are greater.
I've been in Your care all the days of my life.
Forever You will reign.
Eternity and then more do I want to spend with you.

He who holds the universe lives in me.
Even the gates of hell shall not prevail.

Is anything as beautiful as His love?
Should all else fade, His word will still shine.

To God be the glory for all He has done.
One man, His son Jesus, paid for all mankind.

Be assured of who He says you are.
Earth and everything will fade, but He will remain.

Worshiped is what He was, is, and will be.
Only He is perfect and above all.
Run your given race faithfully,
So, at the end, you may hear, "Well done my good and faithful servant."
Hold on tightly to His word and promises.
If you should falter, He will lift you up.
Pray in bad times.
Pray even more in the good times.
El Olam will be with you always.
Do as he commanded and, above all, love first.

Steal My Show

To You be all praise.
To You I'll sing for the rest of my days.
Through the darkest night and morning sun,
You will be the mountain to which I run.
I will keep myself in Your ways.
Should I ever seize to put You first,
Remind me that without You I am cursed.
Help me keep my eyes on you.
It's You I'll hold on to.
For your blessings and mercy do I thirst.
I ask You to make me Your vessel,
Even as my soul and spirit wrestle.
Please guide me towards Your love,
The love that made You come down from Heaven above.
Lord, within Your word is where I'll nestle.
So even though they're all here for me,
Please, Lord, let them see.
Let them see I have done none of this of my own power.
Show them that You are my strong tower.
When it's done help them see that you are on our side and always
will be.

How To Be Great

Love God above all else.
Oh, how simple was the command?
Life is easier than we make it.
Effortless, that's what it should have been.

To serve others.
Oh, humanity why was that so hard?
Damned by foolishness, why did we draw that card?

Awarded is the Kingdom to the servant.
No one shall inherit more than he.
Dispersed to him will the wealth of Heaven be.

Yet, we have gone and reversed it all.
Our idea of great is those who are served.
Unilaterally we spit on the Word.
Rotten have our perceptions become.
No man is greater than the servant in Heaven.
Everlasting shall their wealth be.
In God's eyes, he did what was right.
Grand will his reward be.
Haughtiness did not enter his heart.
Boast only did he of The Lord.
Of nothing shall he lack.
Right with God shall he stand.

Above all, the servant loved God.
Night and day did he seek His word.
Delighted did he exist in The Lord's presence.

Serve, that's all he ever did.
Every night and every day,
Reverently did he pray.
Viciously did he serve and seek The Lord.
Each moment of his life did he live for others.
Above all, he loved God and his neighbor.
Leaving a piece of his heart wherever he went.
Wouldn't it be grand should we all live as he did?
Amazing, that's what this world would be.
Yet it's oh, so terribly sad.
Serving is seen by society as bad.

Even If You Don't

Lord, they asked me why I believe.
Essentially, they questioned my faith,
Attacked my strong tower, but
Don't worry, here's what I said:

Mighty and strong does He stand.
Every tongue confesses the power of His hand.

Through all adversity, He stood with me.
He has never failed, and He won't start now.
Rohi, my shepherd, has always cared for me;
Only He holds the keys.
Unchallenged He reigns.
Grace so freely given;
His love ran red.

Though it may not always seem, so,
He is always working.
Even if the world says not to, I will praise.

Forever I'll love Him, and forever I'll stand.
I'll fight for Him in good times and bad.
Righteous I will run my race, and
Even if serving Him is a crime then a criminal will I be.

Only He deserves all of me.
He is the only one who for me gave it all.

God my Father, that is what I said.
On that day I stood on Your word.
The Book of Daniel said it best of my faith: even if You don't
deliver me from the fire I will still praise You alone.

WORDS OF POWER

Fruits

Love is first above all.
He alone answered the call.
He paid the price for our sins both large and small.
Before Abraham He was.
He died and paid for us with no pause.
Only He had no flaws.
In this action, he gave us a fruit:
This fruit from a tree impossible to uproot;
A fruit whose power none can refute.
The fruit he gave was love,
Love that stands alone and above,
Love purer than the whitest dove.
Upon that mountain, He died to see Satan fall.

Another fruit of ours seems to obey no laws.
Sometimes it seems to have no cause.
Other times it's expressed by applause.
This fruit acts in a power absolute.
It moves in a manner swift and resolute.
Yet this fruit has no institute.
Oh! How wonderful joy is and its cause!

The final fruit is rather astute.
It is the only one capable of rendering everything against it moot.
As proper as it is it could wear a suit.
Maybe it's not something to write of?
Yet, people chase it more than love.
They chase their own peace that will fit like a glove.
Peace, they hope will hold them down like a root.
This fruit is hard to keep a hold of;
It can fly away like the morning dove.
Nonetheless, it is something we love.
Peace, joy, and love – what a massive haul,
The harvest which to collect one must not stall.
They will prevent all stumbles from becoming a fall.

Forgiveness

The hardest thing to do is forgive.
It's nearly as hard to let go.
But to not forgive is to let pain live.
Not letting go only causes divisions of the heart to grow.
Forgiving is the only way to move on and once again live.
Let forgiveness then from every heart flow.

Yet how often should one move on?
The answer is 70 x 7 and then again with each new dawn.
It is better to forgive and to forget.
It is better to let hatred not become set.
Hatred only to dark places is drawn.
It is not like forgiveness; it will make even the best person a pawn.

Hatred will make a pawn of the best.
It will put them in a stranglehold.
That hold will send them to eternal rest.
A rest that will be spitefully cold.
Hatred is not so kind as to grant a final request.
In choosing it over forgiveness their soul they sold.

So, forgiveness may be hard, but it is right.
It is best to forgive and not lose sight.
Hatred though appealing is not good.
Eventually, it cuts the best down as an axe cuts wood.
Forgive then and move toward light!
Take control of the story and what they may write.

Forgive and always fully forget.
Don't give in to hatred, revenge, or regret.
Forgive and always fully forget.

Hunger

Hunger is a funny thing, you know.
Some people it drives mad.
Other people it inspires.
Some it drives to work.
Others it leads to steal.
By most it is despised.
Many have suffered this ill.
Towards it many turn a blind eye.
If only more people would love their neighbor.
The problem is simple to solve.
The first step is the golden rule.
The next and only last step is this:
To live to serve and not be served.
This is the next and only last step.
To solve the problem is simple.
More people would love their neighbor, if only.
Many turn a blind eye towards it.
This ill many have suffered.
It is despised by most.
It leads others to steal.
It drives some to work.
It inspires other people.
It drives some people mad.
You know, hunger is a funny thing.

Grace

It doesn't matter how far you ran.
You need not ponder if it's too late.
What has ever been added by worrying?
Never once has that bought any time.
The thing is that there is one truth:
The truth is that grace wins every time.
Cast away your hurt.
Leave behind your pain.
Allow your scars to fade.
Put down that blade.
Turn your doubt into faith.
The thing is that there is one truth:
The truth is that grace wins every time.
It sets you free.
It's not something you can earn.
You could never have paid the price for it.
This gift was given purely out of love.
Step into it boldly and live under its promise.
Cast off the shame and guilt that tries to hold you down.
The thing is that there is one truth:
The truth is that grace wins every time.
So, you need not care how far you ran.
The Kingdom of Grace has a table for you.
Come into the freedom that's inside.
The truth is that grace wins every time.
The thing is that there is one truth.

Risen

Peace that flows like a river
All at once was bought
In blood that is priceless.
Death was brought to its knees.

In one moment, He died for love.
Now we have a path to God.

For to know Him I will live,
Until my time is done.
Love that's undeniable.
Love greater than all.

Oh, it simply does not make sense.
No, why would my Lord die for me?

Come oh! Come now all to Him,
All that are lost.
Let Him lead you into life.
Victory by his blood was bought.
All of us can know one truth.
Risen is our God.
Yes, risen is our God!

THE MANY
SHADES OF LOVE

Reminiscence

I dream of once again dreaming.
Feeling is all I long after and want.
I remember her wistful and resigned,
Dreaming up thoughts in her colorful mind.
She'd look at the moon and colors speckled her hair.
She'd gaze far away at almost nothing and everything it seemed.
Me? I just made a home in those amber gold eyes of hers as I
dreamed.
This home wasn't perfect nor sound and singing around it no
bird could be found.
Nonetheless, it kept me safe while the clock hands ran, and the
hourglass sand fell.
Time waits for no man, but I wish the old man would have held
then.
Something, anything, just long enough for me to realize I was
losing a friend.
I took one final look into her eyes, and it was as if she held my
soul.
My heart yearned for me to try; my soul knew it had to say
goodbye.
So now it's autumn and the pumpkins ripen and the rabbits are
off to sleep.
Even though I dream of dreaming, I know the time is past.
There's nothing left to feel, or any healing which will last.
I hope she'll remain wistful, resigned, beautiful, and kind.
Maybe someday, somewhere, sometime, there'll be someone as
good as she that I'll call mine.

You and I

You're the whisper of the wind.
I'm the storm of the seas.
Our natures are our bind.
You're the soft summer breeze.
I'm the blistering sun.
Our story would take up too many trees.
You're beautiful and fun.
I'm brusque and strong.
Our attraction makes us become undone.
You're always singing a beautiful song.
I'm the one whose words you spun.
You're always playing with my heart, yet I go along.
I'm just a fool who won't let go.
Our story just keeps running along.
You're the one who made me smile when I felt low.
I'm the coward who decided to run away.
Our separation, however, has helped me grow.
You're no longer the light of my day.
I'm no longer troubled by your memory.
Our lives are better when we both go our own way.
You're not by any means a rarity.

I'm not able to say that I lost much.
Our time spent was wasted, verily.
You're not a loss; I don't know why I treated you as such.
I'm in a league to which you do not pertain.
Our good times to me were nothing more than a crutch.
You're free to live your life going everywhere and starting up a
fire.
I'm free to keep being lightning and sparking hope and progress
wherever I roam.
Our persons are so opposed I don't know why I ever cared for you
like a rose.

Could've, Would've, Should've, Didn't

Was it really love?
It could have been at the time.
Maybe it was lust?
Then why did it feel so good?
Maybe cause we were broken.
We didn't see our pain.
We ignored what was obvious.
We were just passing time.
All that we did was dull our pain.
Funny how we ignored our brains.
Maybe it was love.
At least what we thought it was.
Yet, we were poison.
We were also ecstasy.
Maybe a different time
We may have worked it out.
We may have been able to heal.
We may have moved forward.
Except now it is far too late.
I'm back on stage and you are gone.
I hope you'll heal without me around.
My songs will always carry your sound.

If The Time Had Been Right

They were right; the time was wrong.
It could have all worked out.
Maybe the story would have a different end.
Even now they wonder what could have been.
Who knows?
They were young; the wisdom they needed was far off.
If only they would have waited.
Most likely things would have been different.
Except for their pride, they could have worked.
Couldn't they?
They were fools; the love between them was lost.
In an eye blink, they fell apart.
Mightily they fell.
Elsewhere, in a different place, they both belong.
Where though?
They no longer speak; the pain of loss keeps them apart.
Is it sad what happened between them?
Most days I know at least one of them cries.
Each day one of them thinks to call.
Why don't they?
Don't call, neither one of them answers.
Assuredly we didn't work because the time wasn't right.

To Be a Stranger Again

Your love for him needed no alibI.
Only you held his heart.
Uniquely you saw through his flawS.
Right now, however, you're cold enough to cause hypothermiA.
Even then he still melted when your face he saW.

Now all he can do is watcH.
Oh, he watches your eyes pierce him like needles on cactI.
Those eyes he once loved now kill hiM.

Every day he tries to forgeT.
Ah, but all he does is remembeR.
So many thoughts of you are locked in his memorY.
You are the best part of his past.

To your heart he no longer knows the patH.
Oh, he no longer has eyes to seE.

Full of anguish he is; as to him, you are alooF.
On losing you, he developed insomniA.
Resolute he sits alone waiting for a stimulI.
Gently he cries as he remembers it alL.
Every memory reminds him of his worst liE.
The lie to himself that he only saw you as a frienD.

Contrary Love

The opposite of love is not hate.
It is indifference.
It is a failure to remember the details.
It is forgetting the plans you made.
It is failing to listen.
It is refusing repeatedly to change.
It is being loud about your pain, but ignorant of theirs.
It is threatening to leave instead of learn.
It is choosing others over them.
It is taking what you have for granted.
It is being unwilling, ultimately, to try.
It is ignoring what they care about.
It is sealing emotions away.
It is running when they need you most.
It is being cold and resigned.
The opposite of love is not hate, but when you stop acting on that
loving feeling.
It is being cold and resigned.
It is running when they need you most.
It is sealing your emotions away.
It is ignoring what they care about.
It is being unwilling, ultimately, to try.
It is taking what you have for granted.
It is choosing others over them.
It is threatening to leave instead of learn.

It is being loud about your pain, but ignorant of theirs.
It is refusing, repeatedly, to change.
It is failing to listen.
It is forgetting the plans you made.
It is a failure to remember the details.
It is indifference.
The opposite of love is not hate.

A Rival

Faith, trust: it was worth it.

It was worth each second, believe me.

It was only after the fact that I would see.

Being your rival was fun, I admit.

The experience taught me a great many lessons in determination and grit.

At the time we both argued about who we could be.

In the end, we could never agree.

We never agreed, just argued tooth and bit.

We were rivals in that short time.

Even though I never said it, I admired you.

I admired you, and you pushed me to climb.

You pushed me to find successes and victories anew.

I hope our rivalry for you also had some rhyme.

Faith, I never said it, but in our rivalry part of me fell in love with you.

The Time of Leaving and Forgetting

It's only a matter of time till you leave.
You're too much of a coward to wear your heart on your sleeve.
Darling, can't you see that our love is doomed?
Whatever passion we had for each other was consumed.
I wish I could ignore the obvious and be naïve.
I wish this was something I didn't believe.
Your actions leave me nothing else to perceive.
Long have I thought of your leaving and assumed;
It's only a matter of time.
I'll soon at your leaving be caused to grieve.
You'll soon go find someone else to deceive.
Maybe you loved me once in that spring when the flowers
bloomed,
Now that love has been entombed.
Soon our lives shall no longer interweave.
It's only a matter of time.
In time you'll forget the love I gave to you.
You'll forget me as you lie to someone new.
You'll tell them they have your heart.
You'll tell them they're a work of art.
You'll lie as you always do.
The words from your mouth will not be true.

Then you'll cast them aside and look for a better view.
Then once you find it from them, you'll depart.
In time you'll forget.
You'll forget all the love that was ever given to you.
I hope you find yourself hopeless as to what you should do.
I hope that then you fall apart.
Fall apart recognizing that you can't restart.
Yet I know my wish won't come true, because just like you
always do.
In time you'll forget.
It's only a matter of time till you forget and leave like you
always do.

Dove

I looked right into your eyes.
Lost myself within their skies.
And as you looked back at me.
It was almost like a dream.
Because when you looked right at me,
I could clearly see your heart.
Then you pulled yourself away,
And I was the one to blame.

Now I lie here wondering
What has become of your smile.
Wondering what I could have done to see you smile just for a
while.

Then again, I know it's true.
I didn't tell you the truth.
I was just a scared young man.
I saw my shadow and I ran.

I wish I would have shown you
The truth from the very start.
The truth is that I was me,
And you were a work of art.

I tried to cover up my scars,
Tried to be who I once was.
But I just pushed you away.
I never meant to cause you pain.

Simple but Impactful

Maybe to you, it was just a dance.
To you, they were simply flowers.
For you, the time we shared was only passing hours.
Maybe to you, they were only passing words.
To you, they didn't mean much.
For you, it was a small act and you treated it as such.
It wasn't small to me.
For me, it was you showing you cared.
You were vulnerable, if only for a second.
That was unfamiliar territory we both stepped in.
I let myself be cared for and you didn't shy away.
For me it was an unfamiliar feeling.
You were there, and then gone.
That was a sad moment we both came upon.
I let myself be cared for, and that was huge to me;
Nonetheless, it was small to you.
Maybe to you, it meant nothing.
To you, they were just empty moments.
For you, we might as well have been opponents.
Maybe to you, it didn't mean anything.
To you, it meant nothing when you said, "I love you."
For you, the words' weight was small and untrue.
It wasn't small to me.

The Unlived Moments

It's not the past you miss, but what could have been.
You miss that which you never had.
You regret what you couldn't begin.
The simple realization of what never was is sad.
It's a song meant for the world's smallest violin.
It's odd missing what never was.
Even worse is imagining what never will be.
Sadder yet is you know you fell apart, but don't know the cause.
It's honestly tragic, the pain you hold.
Now you just reminisce about a future you won't see.
Now you just let your heart turn cold.
It's true that it's better to try and fail;
At least you allowed yourself to be bold.
You gave your best to no avail.
Yes, you do not miss what once was.
No, you miss the future you didn't get to live.
In the end, you miss the small moments when it all seemed to fade.
You miss the ones that never will be again.
After all, you miss all that was and all that could have been.

Uncommon Parallels

The heart begins to race.
The breath begins to slow.
The body begins to quiver at a slow tempo.
Within the mind, a storm starts to brew.
A flood of emotions drowns out reality.
For a moment, the ephemeral seems eternal;
In the eternal, the abstract becomes concrete;
The formless begins to take shape.
That shape is one both unfamiliar and somehow safe.
Within the midst of the uncertainty, everything starts to race
along with the heart.
Within the moment breath has slowed to a stop.
As time passes, the body starts to still.
In a moment, the mental hurricane ceases.
The flood sufficiently covered existence.
What could once only be felt now has a shape to touch.
The only question that remains is this:
Is this the moment before love or before death?

Turn To Me

If you can't see the sunshine, I'll be your light.
Turn to me.
Should the clouds cover your light, I'll shine for you instead.
Turn to me.
If rain should fall and you can't hide, let me shelter you.
Turn to me.
Should everything seem chaotic, let me be your calm.
Turn to me.

THE ANIMALS

Not Just a Dog

They're not just dogs. How can you say that?
I defy you to say it again!
Just a dog! The audacity of you!
They are more friends than you ever were.
Where were you when life crushed my soul?
They were there, they saw all my pain.
What about the tears no one else heard?
Oh wait! They heard them, for they were there.
Where were you when I needed your time?
You weren't there, but they helped me move on.
What jokes do we share for us and no one else?
They knew my life, they were family.
Where is this peace you tell me I'll find?
My peace was with them, and now they are gone.
So please, don't insult me with your flippant words that
patronize my soul.
Cause I am burying a beloved part of me.
And no, they weren't a pet, they were a part of me I won't soon
forget.

Nature's Alarm

They sing at daybreak.
Their song sings the world awake.
Quiet and calm chirps,
Soft, beautiful, calming songs.
Though they could fly far and free,
For a moment they stop.
They rest to sing their song to us,
A gift given freely.
We can learn from their harmony.
We learn from their harmony.
We learn to slow down and listen.
Listen to the calm.
Take a moment to just breathe.
Step back for a bit.
Relax and let the calm flow.
For a moment just exist.
There's a reason they sing.
They do it to share their freedom,
To let us fly with them.
Their song lets us know we're all right,
Reminds us that there is still light.
The birds sing their song and christen the new day,
Nature's alarm so we don't waste it away.

Dogged

People fight as you teach them. They do.
Teach them like a wolf then.
Remind them they should always protect the pack.
Show them that they should run and not quit.
Show them patience is a virtue.
Teach them to think and then act.
Remind them that silence is strength.
See, wolves know this all too well.
Working in teams they succeed.
Their leaders lead by example.
For one and for all is how they fight.
Most important of all: they're loyal.
If people mirrored wolves the world would be better.
They're loyal most important of all.
They fight for one and for all.
They lead by example, their leaders.
They succeed working in teams.
Wolves know this all too well, see.
Silence is strength: remind them.
Think and then act: teach them.
Patience is a virtue: show them.
They should run and not quit: show them that.
They should always protect the pack: remind them.
Then teach them like a wolf.
They do fight as you teach them, people.

The Jungle's King

You're not the largest.
You'll never be the fastest.
Your wit is easily outmatched.
In fact, you sleep more than almost anyone.
Oddly enough, you're not even the strongest.
Your glare, though intimidating, is not quite piercing.
Your roar is strong, but not the loudest.
Ironically, your bite, though feared, is weak compared to others.
Somehow, you're still called king.
Yes, Mr. Lion, we humans could learn a great deal from you.
We could learn to focus on our strengths instead of our
weaknesses.
Having half your patience and accuracy would serve us well.
Knowing when to rest and when to act as you do is a skill.
Yes, not because of what you do wrong but what you do right the
truth is this:
Somehow, you're still called king.

Over Mountains and Forests and Seas

Only one avian elicits such wonder,
Whether it be because of flight
Or its cry soft as the thunder.
The eagle captures the mind and sight.
Soaring a nearly boundless height,
It views the world that is under
Its high and soaring might.
Only one avian elicits such wonder,
The eagle whom none can plunder.
The majestic eagle of flight.
The eagle standard of wonder.
Whether it be because of flight,
Or its coat shimmering in the light.
This avian is a strong hunter.
Yes, always ready for the fight
Or its cry soft as the thunder.
Maybe that's what makes it stronger.
The fact that its cry causes fright—
Perhaps that is why it does not go under.
The eagle captures mind and sight.
It soars to awe-striking heights
Over the world, giving cover.
Giving cover as it takes flight.
The eagle is as mighty as thunder.
Only one avian elicits such wonder.

EL PASO

The Star

You're invisible at day,
Yet we know you're there.
Come night you will shine once again.
Then all will see you, my dear friend,
You bright Mountain Star.
How bright and visible you are,
Shining for all to see.
It's a wonder how many dreams you've set free.
You're invisible at day,.
Almost as if you're power was meant to be at bay.
If you shone at day you'd compete with the sun;
Yet, the sun never made so many dreams run.
You bright Mountain Star.
Keep on shining near and far.
Lead us to the hopes and dreams on the mountain where you are.

City of All Seasons

Here I've lived all my youth.
Fear not I say the truth.
Each year this city does something magical;
Speech has no words to describe the spectacle.
City of all seasons, that's what I say,
Pretty amazing that I can witness this each year, each day.
Blistering summers led to the Sun City name,
Whispering winds through the summer whose heat they tame.
Chilled autumns with short days and long memories,
Filled are those autumns with a great many told stories.
From autumn winter is born.
Some people begin their houses to adorn.
Spring comes after the winter's thaw.
The birds sing telling us what they saw.
All the seasons give this city a visit come year's end.
Small wonder, not many people notice the trend.
Yet, no matter how many times this all happens that I see,
Set, as the trend may be,
Bet, it's always just as beautiful to me.
Let me not forget the yearly majesty.

The Invisible Landmark

We seldom miss you till you're gone,
Drawn away with someplace else to be.
Free and voiceless as the dawn,
Don and master of what we can't see.
Spree and beautiful you stand as a swan.
Foregone is the conclusion of your breeze to me;
Trees and mountains stop you from keeping on.
Brawn and weakness are spirited within thee.
When you're rash, you'll bury our town in dust;
Cussed in that time is your name then.
Again, you would abandon our trust.
Lust to destroy in anger a hundred men.
Zen and peace in your storms you bust.
Must you write your story so foully with your pen;
For all your bad, however, you do have good.
You cool and protect from blistering heat.
Sweet is your breeze that blows true.
Few feelings this one can beat.
Treat us always with soft breezes anew.
Then I believe this is your judgment:
You're an invisible landmark and one that we need;
Your purpose can only be fulfilled by you indeed.

The Lights

Inspiring, I guess that is the right word.
Yes, it's a fine one indeed.
Inspiration is a power greater than any sword.
They're more powerful than most.
They break dark.
Dark they break.
They turn it into a ghost.
They shine bright.
Bright they shine.
Yes, more powerful than most.
You see, something as powerful as they cannot long be ignored.
Sooner or later, they'll be freed
To be abhorred or adored.
They're creators in their right.
They birth sight.
Sight they birth.
They make it reality.
They give life.
Life they give.

Yes, creators in their right.
The lights that draw us forward.
The lights from which we recede.
The lights in which all memory is stored.
They are strong and fleeting too.
They can die.
Die they can.
They may die, but usually
They live on.
On they live.
Yes, they are strong and fleeting.

Shining Just for Me

As I sit on this mountain, I look out upon the city I love and its great wide expanse.
I see a million hearts filled with a million dreams,
Dreams that so many chase after, but few attain.
Attaining dreams is harder than dreaming them.
Yet, maybe, if everyone could see what I see as I sit on this mountain;
Maybe, just maybe things would be different.
As I sit on this mountain, I see one of my city's unsung beauties:
Those lights that shine over those million hearts and dreams.
Yes, in these lights I can see a bright hope for all of them.
I can see all the dreams which became realities in each of those lights.
Then I imagine each of those representing a dream that has been lived.
As I sit on this mountain and look at these lights, I am sure
One day far off someone else will sit on this mountain as I do now.
They'll look out upon the city I love and its great wide expanse.
I hope that when they do, they'll see a million hearts and dreams as I do now.
I hope that they see the light that represents the dream I dreamed.
Then maybe they'll have the same one-worded thought that I have now, "Wow!"

A Message to the Fence

You're the one landmark of this city I despise.
You hurt my eyes and darken my day.
A permanent stay and reminder of a pointless division.
You're a physical definition of hate,
A visible mate and partner of disdain.
Yes, an eyesore and pain running for miles,
All the while splitting people who could be allies.
So, yes, you're a landmark I despise, Mr. Fence;
With a passion deep and immense I despise your existence.

I KNEW THEM ONCE

Day 1

Do they matter to you?
Um, truly, honestly, I don't know anymore.
Maybe you knew them once?
You said it: I did know them, just not right now.
Well, exactly what happened?
I can't speak for them, but I'll tell you, my part.

I made the mistake of lying to them and myself.
How did you manage that?
As always, I acted, even made them think I cared.
That's them, what about you?
My lie to myself: believing they cared for me.
You're still hiding something.
Ah, yes, I'm hiding why I decided to leave.
Well, why did you, my friend?
I'll tell you tomorrow, I promise; but right now, it's rather late.
Tomorrow, you have got it, just don't be late.
I won't be, I never am, not if there's a story to tell.
Okay then, this place tomorrow, at noon I hope you'll tell the
story well.

Day 2

Well, you're on time, shall we start?
As I said, I'm never late to tell a story.
Then, tell me your story.
Well, since you're the first person to listen, here goes.

I left them behind because I loved someone.
I thought you didn't care.
You're right, I didn't care about them, but someone else.
Who was this someone then?
I won't give you her name; it would be too unfair.
Fine, who was she to you?
To me, she was worth enough to give up on them.
A girl—that's why you left?
The people I called friends, well one broke her heart.
How did they manage that?
For that answer, you'll have to come meet me here again
tomorrow.
Well, I already came here twice what will thrice visiting matter?
So, you'll be here I presume?
Yes, as yesterday and today, I'll be here to hear your story in this
café at noon.

Day 3

Today, you're a bit late.
Noon seemed a bit too soon, so I came at five past.
Well, that seems fair enough.
Now, to tell you how he managed to break her heart.

He broke her heart by lying about who he was.
Let me guess, just like you?
In a way, but not exactly. Different somehow.
Different exactly how?
His lust led him to lie and fake about his love.
So, he wasn't honest?
No, he lied about his faith and what he wanted.
Did she learn of the lies?
Not exactly, more that he couldn't lie for long.
What of when she found out?
Since I was late, I'll give you that story today.

I wasn't there when she found out exactly.

Who told you the story?

She did one night, a night we both shared just talking.

What did she tell you then?

That he made her feel worthless when she said no.

No to what exactly?

No to denying her faith, no to sex, no to him.

She chose to be herself.

Yes, but that choice and losing him; that's what broke her.

Yet, she had to do it.

Yes, because he made her feel worthless, not beautiful.

I still have one question.

I'm pretty sure I know what, but go ahead: tell me.

What part do you come in?

The part that you'll have to come tomorrow to hear.

Alright tomorrow, but instead of noon meet me at three.

Three it is so I can tell you about her and me.

Yes, tomorrow that part then the next day you tell me about you and the friends you left.

That sounds good to me. The next two days at three each with a coffee and a story to share between you and me.

Day 4

Three O'clock, this is new.
New is good, new is different. Let us begin.
Tell me where you came in.
It was not I who entered her life, but she mine.

I'll remember the events of that day always.
Always: that's a long time.
Yes, it's the time that measures feelings of the heart.
My question still remains.
We had talked before, but this night was different.
So, you opened your heart?
She and I both did at the time. We both felt safe.
Did you trust each other?
Yes, enough to share secrets we had kept too long.
Yet, you didn't dive in?
I was afraid of loving too hard and too fast.
You feared it couldn't last.
Yes, we acted like we were something we were not.
So, it went up in flames?
Exactly, we both got tired playing the game.

So as for she and I, that's all there is to tell right now.
That's her, what of your friends?
I promise you that tomorrow for the story's end.
Okay, I'll be here then.
Tell me something in truth: have you liked the story?
Well, I've come here everyday have I not?
True. I guess you must be enjoying it then.
It provides me something to recall at day's end.
In that case, I'll see you tomorrow at three for the finale.

Finale

Time for one last story.
Yes, to tell you what became of me and my friends.
I have waited too long.
Hopefully, the story would have been worth your time.

You asked me of them once. Do you recall my words?
You said you knew them once.
Do you remember what I said about them past that?
You didn't know them any more.
Good, because the truth is I no longer know them.
What happened led to that?
There was nothing to reconcile when it was done.
You know that, or you think?
I know because of how I changed, who I became.
I guess you still miss them.
I miss who I thought they could be, not who they are.
Then, it's time to move on.
Well, now that someone else shares my story I can.
Huh, so this is the end.
I guess so, I have no more stories to tell you.
Maybe another time.
Maybe life will give me one in time; then I'll call.

Well, my friend, thank you for the story and this week.
Thank you for listening.
When life gives you another story to tell, call me.
Don't worry. Surely, I will.
What you told me at the beginning then is true.
What of all that I told?
What you said about them and you, past and present.
In reference to your first question, is that what you mean?
Yes, exactly, that's what I mean.
My response to your question if I knew them now satisfies?
Yes, it's true that you knew them once, but not now.
Until life gives you the next story, I guess this is goodbye.
Goodbye until then, please wait for my call.

THE STORY OF
WRITING

I Can't Seem to Write Today

Yesterday my pen had a mind of its own.
Yesterday my pen ran wild with thought.
Oh, yesterday my pen wrote wonderful words.
Today, however, those words are gone.
I can't seem to write today.

Believe me: I have ideas of what to say.
It's just they all come and go;
None of them stay.
I can't seem to write today.

Should I write of love?
Maybe I could write of pain?
How about nature?
Maybe something playful and vain?
I could write about the time I'm wasting.
I could personify the time as a passing train.
Well, confound it, there are too many ideas inside my brain.
I can't seem to write today.

Even if I could settle on a theme, what of structure?
Sonnet, villanelle, free, terza rima, haiku—how could I choose
simply one to do?
I don't think I could even if I tried.
So, I try to think of some thoughts of what to do.
No new thoughts form though, and I quit trying to decide what
to say.
I can't seem to write today.

Whatever I needed to say today will go unsaid.
I'll lay my tired pen to bed.
I can't seem to write today, and I've decided, that's okay.

If I Was a Poet

If only I was a poet.
They can be blunt and misunderstood.
They can invoke emotions both horrible and good.
Could I be a poet? Who knows?
Would I if I could? is a better question I suppose.
The answer to that question I will not expose.
What good are my words if I can't turn them into art?
They're useless and have no worth.
What are my words if not ramblings from which emotions cannot start?
They're useless as words turned to ash at the bottom of a hearth.
If only I was a poet,
Then I could say the things I truly feel.
Then I could avoid saying the words of men who kneel.
An appeal is not something my words have.
Real boredom is all they can invoke.
Please don't ask me why.
I can't seem to answer, no matter how hard I try.
What sadness consumes me as I write?
What pain consumes me as I recognize my lack of skill today?
For as much as I write none of it comes out as I wish it might!
I'm consumed by thinking of all I would say!
If I was a poet.
If only I was a poet.

Not A Poem

What you're reading now is not a poem.
In fact, they are only words.
They are words with no structure.
They do not tell a story, but they are free.
Don't look here for patterns, because they don't exist.
You'd just waste time on a pointless analysis.
These words are not a poem.
They are not anything at all.
In fact, they're just a jumbled-up mess
With no purpose in this whole world.
I don't know why you have kept on reading them.
They are useless, fruitless, and a waste.
What you're reading is a waste of time.
It's just rambling: simple as that.
Why, you could better use your time playing with a cat.
How could this be a poem? It has no rhyme.
Every tune it tries to sing just comes out flat.
It's more useless than a floor-mat.
What you have read is not a poem.
In fact, they were wasted words;
They had no discernible structure;
They did not tell a story, but they are free.
Whatever patterns you may have found were not meant to exist.
You only wasted time on a pointless poem and your analysis.

An Author's Signoff

There was no way I could have imagined any of this.
The truth is I'm simply not that creative.
In actuality, I started writing with no plan in mind.
If any of these words now matter it's not because of me.
To acknowledge everyone who gave these words meaning is
something I must do.
To everyone that inspired me I give thanks;
For through you these words have been immortalized.
For through you I was emboldened to write what I may have hid
away.
To the readers of these words, I give a charge.
Take action with these words and spread them.
Send them off; send them far.
I wrote them; I gave them to you.
I trust all of you to take good care of them.
For what was hidden in my soul is now public and in your care.
May you always be blessed and prosper.
I hope that we can all meet again soon,
Hopefully with some new stories to tell.
Yes, definitely with stories to tell!
Most definitely with stories to tell!
Connect all the underlined letters for one final message.

Facebook: https://www.facebook.com
/share/CAqu51dPSmXzjtDu/?mibex
tid=qi2Omg
Instagram: @LightningPublications
Twitter: @LightningPub18
Email: cordero1804@gmail.com

www.ingramcontent.com/pod-product-compliance
Lightning Source LLC
LaVergne TN
LVHW092323080426
835508LV00039B/513